T0124244

The Daniel Fast Prayer Guide

for

A Personal Prayer Revival

D. Tony and Kathy M. Willis

A 21-day prayer resource to turn your Daniel fast into a personal prayer revival

authorHOUSE®

AuthorHouse™
1663 Liberty Drive
Bloomington, IN 47403
www.authorhouse.com
Phone: 1 (800) 839-8640

Published by AuthorHouse 07/22/2016

ISBN: 978-1-5246-1946-6 (sc)
ISBN: 978-1-5246-1945-9 (e)

Library of Congress Control Number: 2016911813

Print information available on the last page.

Any people depicted in stock imagery provided by Thinkstock are models, and such images are being used for illustrative purposes only. Certain stock imagery © Thinkstock.

This book is printed on acid-free paper.

Unless otherwise indicated, Bible quotations are taken from The King James Version.

Dedication

We dedicate this book to our spiritual family at Soul's Harbor Church of God. Thank you for eagerly participating in the Daniel fast using this prayer guide. Your positive feedback has inspired us to share it with others.

Acknowledgements

We would like to thank Senior Pastor Robert Vance for introducing us to the prayer revival concept very early in our ministry.

I am forever indebted to Pastor Larry Sluder. He served as my mentor in early ministry. He taught me the importance of fasting with a purpose. I pay tribute and honor to him for greatly influencing me, and shaping my ministry.

Special thanks to Madilee C. Wnek. You have the God given talent to take a rough manuscript, shape it, and transform it into a book that can bless others.

Thanks to the many prayer warriors and authors whose books have deepened our spiritual lives and inspired us to write on prayer.

Contents

Introduction

As he scanned the horizon, he could see the terrible destruction. Armed soldiers stood over their victims. Flames ascended as buildings burned and crumbled. What he heard was equally disturbing. Fearful cries from panicked friends and family filled the air. His thoughts raced. Would he be the next to die? A teenager should never have to witness events like these, nor have to think about an uncertain future. His nation had been invaded. Attempts to resist the enemy had failed. Prophets had warned it would happen. Now it was a reality. His country had been destroyed.

Young Daniel discovered he would live, but would be a prisoner of Babylon. As he and his countrymen made their way to a strange new land, their captors asked them to sing a song. Musicians had been allowed to take their harps with them, but they were too distraught to sing (Psalm 137). Once in Babylon, their enslavers gave them new responsibilities. They had to adapt to new customs and a new language. They had to use their skills and talents to benefit this new country. The book of Daniel begins at this point.

Daniel entered Babylon as a teenager. He never returned to his homeland. He rebounded from being abducted, and from the horrors he had witnessed. He even prospered (Daniel 6:28). History would soon reveal that Daniel lived a long life in Babylon, serving several Kings. The book of Daniel details some of his breathtaking experiences, while showing his coping mechanism, his survival technique, and his political advancement.

Fasting and praying helped Daniel to cope, to survive, and to prosper. Christians today still face spiritual challenges, and have learned to do what Daniel did. He set an example with his fasting and praying for 21 days that many churches across America are following. Known as "The Daniel Fast", this yearly church emphasis is usually held in January.

Maintaining spiritual focus is one of many challenges of fasting and praying for three straight weeks. This book provides a daily prayer guide, along with insight to assist you in your personal prayer revival. We hope that this book will be a valuable resource as you seek a closer walk with God through your Daniel fast.

Part One

The Daniel Fast Story

"Pastor, I'm fasting." That statement did not bring the response I expected. He said, "Why are you fasting?" I had a quick answer, "Because you asked the church to fast this week." Then he said something that was simple, but profound. "When you fast, it is good to have a purpose for your fast!" I had expected appreciation and affirmation. After all, I was following the direction he had given the church. He chose to use my declaration as a teachable moment. How easy it would have been for that pastor to feel the support from his congregation and to have said, "Good for you! I'm glad you are participating; we need more young Christians to fast." Instead, he chose to mentor me and to teach me a valuable lesson. That simple exchange has motivated me always to examine why I am fasting.

This pastor's question to me could well be addressed to all those who fast. Often, people who attend a church follow the leadership's challenge for a fast, but do so without a purpose in their hearts. They know it is a good thing to do, and they want to show support. Unfortunately, the main concern when approaching a fast seems to have become, "what can I eat or not eat on this fast?" Many books already explain the food issue, but, often the most important question-- "Why are you fasting?"--goes unanswered.

Biblical fasts always had a purpose, such as in these examples:

1. Ezra fasted for direction and protection (Ezra 8).
2. Nehemiah fasted and prayed because he received bad news about his homeland (Nehemiah 1).
3. A wicked king proclaimed a fast because he was told his nation would be destroyed (Jonah 3).
4. Jehoshaphat proclaimed a fast because Judah was about to be invaded (2 Chronicles 20).
5. The Jews fasted because Esther realized her people would be destroyed (Esther 4).

Daniel's fasting serves as another good example. The book of Daniel describes various times that he fasted and explains why. A close examination of Daniel's fasting reveals he approached his fasts with a great purpose in his heart.

Daniel had been reading the writings of Jeremiah. He understood that the time of the Babylonian captivity was almost over (Daniel 9:1-2). He decided to seek the Lord for understanding about this matter and about the Jewish people's returning home. Daniel was motivated to fast and pray for the future of his people. In response, God sent him a vision and a special angelic appearance (Daniel 10). Daniel had fasted and prayed for 21 days. The angel told him God had heard his petition the first day, and gave him a behind-the-scenes revelation of what had been happening for three weeks. The answer to his prayer had been delayed by spiritual warfare in the heavens. This revelation reminds us that we must have a fierce tenacity as we war against principalities and powers. The angel touched Daniel, and he was able to get on his knees and the palms of his hands (Daniel 10:10). He received a second touch that enabled him to speak (Daniel 10:16). He received a third touch that gave him strength (Daniel 10:18). The angel revealed he had been sent to disclose the future of Israel (Daniel 10:14). Daniel fasted and prayed for 21 days to understand what would happen to his people. The purpose of his fast is revealed to us. God honored his fasting and prayer, and gave him what he sought.

Our participation in a 21-day Daniel fast will, obviously, have a different purpose. Before participating in this fast, we should consider what we want God to do, thinking carefully about why we are spending 21 days to humble ourselves and seek Him. We saw some earlier examples that taught us why several people fasted. My pastor's question is still very relevant: "Why are you fasting?"

Another matter to consider in participating relates to health issues. Some people must eat to avoid a life-threatening crisis. Still others say they eat so little that doing without food is "no big deal". So the question arises, "Pastor, how can I participate in the church fast?" Testimonies have illustrated that a different method of fasting may be more beneficial for these folks. For instance, some say they feel addicted to social media, entertainment, sports, or hobbies. Such admissions reveal that these activities may be hurting them spiritually, so they have chosen to abstain from those things during the Daniel fast. Many have testified that participating in the Daniel fast has greatly helped them in their area of struggle. You will find many books and resources dedicated to the "How to Fast" subject, but this book will focus on the purpose of fasting, as well as provide you with a prayer guide for your fast.

The Daniel Fast Prayer Guide

A 21-day Daniel fast requires discipline. It also requires focus. Though we fast with a spiritual purpose, we sometimes lack focus in our daily prayers. Many who participate do not need prayer assistance. However, others welcome help to make the Daniel fast more meaningful and rewarding. The goal of this Daniel fast prayer guide is to help us maintain focus while praying. The guide has a weekly and a daily prayer emphasis. The weekly emphasis is taken from this prayer that Jesus prayed.

> "*Our Father which art in heaven, Hallowed be thy name. Thy kingdom come. Thy will be done in earth, as it is in heaven. Give us this day our daily bread. And forgive us our debts, as we forgive our debtors. And lead us not into temptation, but deliver us from evil: For thine is the kingdom, and the power, and the glory, for ever. Amen.*" (Matthew 6:9-13).

This lesson teaches us our prayers should be a time of worshipping God, of praying about our needs, and of interceding for others. These three lessons from Jesus will serve as our weekly emphasis. The prayer guide will begin with a week of upward focus on worship. The second week will have an inward focus, as we pray about our needs. In our final week, we will direct our focus outwardly, praying for others. So our prayers will have an upward look, an inward look, and an outward look.

The Daniel fast prayer guide is designed to assist with your daily prayers. All 21 days have an important prayer emphasis. The emphasis will help focus our daily prayers. We strongly recommend that you read the second part of this book in its entirety before you begin your Daniel fast. Doing so will make your time of fasting and prayer much more rewarding and will give you a greater understanding of the prayer guide.

For the next 21 days, the prayer guide will have specific directions for your daily prayer. These brief suggestions will help you grow in your prayer life. They are designed to be a small part of your daily prayer, serving as a source of inspiration to assist you with the Daniel fast. You will notice many scriptures that encourage kneeling to pray; but of course, the main thing is that you spend time in prayer during your fast.

WEEK ONE

This week we will focus on the first part of the prayer Jesus used to teach his disciples: "Hallowed be thy name." Jesus began this lesson on prayer by offering worship to his Father. For the next seven days, our daily prayer will focus on various aspects of worshipping God.

<u>Day One</u>: Kneel Before the Lord Our Maker

The Bible gives us a wonderful invitation to bow before the Lord in prayer. Psalm 95:6 reads, "O come, let us worship and bow down: let us kneel before the Lord our maker." Scripture tells us "It is he that hath made us and not we ourselves" (Psalm 100:3).

Adam and Eve both knew the source of their lives. Adam may have looked at the dirt beneath his feet and realized he was made out of it. He knew that God fashioned him and breathed the breath of life into his body. Though far removed from the place where God created man, we must never be far removed from recognizing he is our source of life. It is with great gratitude we worship and bow before the Lord, our creator.

Day Two: Kneel to Enthrone Him as Your God

The Bible shows us many who were torn between different gods. Elijah told the children of Israel, that they were halting between God and Baal (1 Kings 18:21). Joshua declared that the people "should put away the gods" (Joshua 24:14). He told Israel he and his house had chosen to serve God (Joshua 24:15).

David sang, "I will praise thee, O Lord <u>my</u> God..." (Psalms 86:12a). Again we see David saying, "The Lord is <u>my</u> light and <u>my</u> salvation..." (Psalms 27:1a). (Underscoring added) We kneel today acknowledging that we have chosen Jehovah as our God. There is no other god before him. We enthrone him as our God.

Day Three: Kneel to Show Reverence and Honor

We kneel before the Lord to reverence him and to show honor. His word acknowledges that the whole world will one day kneel before him to show reverence and honor. Isaiah 45:23 reads, "I have sworn by myself, the word is gone out of my mouth in righteousness, and shall not return, That unto me every knee shall bow, every tongue shall swear." The New Testament shows kings kneeling before Jesus: "... they fell down, and worshipped him..." (Matthew 2:11). We humbly bow today to show reverence and honor.

Day Four: Kneel to Celebrate the Power of God

Jesus prayed acknowledging the power of God. "For thine is the kingdom, and the power, and the glory, forever, Amen." (Matthew 6:13b). Jesus also acknowledged that "All power is given unto me in heaven and in earth." (Matthew 28:18b). God's power formed the worlds. His power parted the Red Sea for the children of Israel. Through his power we have life. We know he has the power to meet our needs and to answer our prayers. We rejoice in his great power.

Day Five: Kneel to Celebrate the Love of God

John the apostle often wrote about the love of God. In John 3:16 he wrote, "For God so loved the world that he gave his only begotten Son..." We see God's love for us expressed through the death of Jesus upon the cross. He also wrote, "God is love," (1 John 4:8b). His word reveals that he is full of loving kindness, and that he is longsuffering towards us. We are the objects of God's great love, kindness, and patience. We joyfully kneel to worship God for the great love he has bestowed upon us.

Day Six: Kneel to Celebrate His Mercy and Grace

Noah was one of the first men to ever discover the wonder of the grace of God. As the rain descended and the flood raged, he no doubt thanked God that he had received grace (Genesis 6:8). We acknowledge his grace and mercy has been given to us as we kneel before him. Paul wrote, "… by grace ye are saved." (Ephesians 2:5b). He also wrote about the mercy of God, "… according to his mercy he saved us…" (Titus 3:5b). We worship him for his grace and mercy; without which we would be forever lost.

<u>Day Seven</u>: Kneel to Worship and Give Thanks

The Bible shows Mary the sister of Lazarus at the feet of Jesus on three occasions. In Luke 10:39 she sat at his feet and listened to him teach. In John 11:32, while grieving for her dead brother, Mary fell down at the feet of Jesus. On the third occasion we see Mary kneeling before Jesus to anoint him with a pound of expensive spikenard ointment (John 12:3). She knelt worshipping the one who had raised her brother back to life.

The original meaning of the word "worship" is "worth-ship". Bowing before the Lord in prayer is an act that shows our affection and love. Psalm 95:6 says, "O come, let us worship and bow down: let us kneel before the Lord our maker." A song writer once wrote, "Enter into his gates with thanksgiving, and into his courts with praise: be thankful unto him, and bless his name." (Psalm 100:4).

WEEK TWO

Our daily prayer for the week will focus on the second part of our Lord's prayer. Jesus prayed for the Father to supply the need for daily bread. He also prayed that we would not enter into temptation, but be delivered from evil. We see Jesus teaching us to pray for ourselves.

We are encouraged to ask, to seek, and to knock. Our daily prayer will focus on our relationship with God, and upon God's meeting our needs.

<u>Day Eight</u>: Kneel to Celebrate Your Connection to God

Just before Jesus went to the cross, he talked about his connection to the Father and to his children. While the Father is the husbandman, Jesus is the vine and we are the branches (John 15:1-6). Salvation connects us to God, making us part of the family of God. The Bible tells us that sin separates us from God. Isaiah wrote, "But your iniquities have separated between you and your God, and your sins have hid his face from you, that he will not hear." (Isaiah 59:2). The Psalmist let us know that sin hinders our prayer:

"If I regard iniquity in my heart, the Lord will not hear me." (Psalm 66:18).

The Old Testament often presents the picture of Israel as a sinful nation that needed to repent and return to him. The reconnecting of Israel brought God's presence, protection, and favor.

As we kneel before the Lord, we should examine our hearts. If our hearts reveal that we have sinned, we should quickly repent of that sin. We must make sure we are connected to God, and we should celebrate being joined to the Father. Jesus did. He prayed saying that he and the Father were one (John 17:21).

Day Nine: Kneel and Pray to Be Fruitful

Jesus taught us that branches that are connected to the vine will be productive. The husbandman shapes the branches so that they will bare much fruit. When we think about God working in our lives to make us fruitful, we realize he is shaping us to be productive.

As we think about serving Him, we recognize we should pray that he will reveal how we can be fruitful. We kneel in prayer to discover our gifts, to develop our gifts, and to deploy our gifts. God will place us in the right spot, and give us opportunities to bear much fruit.

Day Ten: Kneel as an Act of Submission

Every Christian should strive to do the will of the Father. We see Jesus kneeling before the Father in the Garden of Gethsemane and submitting his will to the Father. Three times Jesus prayed to surrender his will to the Father, and that the Father's will would be done (Matthew 26:39).

There will be times in our lives when we struggle to obey the Lord. We must strive to completely surrender to him, denying ourselves and taking up our cross to follow him (Matthew 16:24). We are to submit our ways to him. The bible says, "Trust in the Lord with all thine heart; and lean not unto thine own understanding. In all thy ways acknowledge him, and he shall direct thy paths." (Proverbs 3:5,6). He is the good shepherd who guides his sheep. We kneel, as Jesus knelt, to submit ourselves to the will of the Father, and to receive his direction for our lives.

Day Eleven: Kneel to Pray for Physical Needs

At times we may face physical issues. This serves to remind us that we are all susceptible to sickness. But, the Bible tells us that God has provided healing when sickness comes. Simon Peter told us that Christ had stripes placed on his back for our healing (1 Peter 2:24).

Having the physical ability to actively serve God requires good health. A pastor who has a health problem struggles to have the strength to visit, to serve as an administrator, and to prepare sermons. All those who serve God need strength and healing.

Our prayer is that God would give us good health. If we have sickness we pray for healing. We seek him for his constant strength that enables us to serve. In Mark 1:40 we see a sick man kneeling before the Lord. Jesus answered his prayer for healing and made him whole.

Day Twelve: Kneel to Pray to Be a Faithful Steward

Stewardship is like being a manager. Such a person is responsible for assuring the company runs smoothly. The owner has entrusted his company into the manager's hands. Joseph serves as a good example. Potiphar delegated the keeping of his house to Joseph (Genesis 39:3-4). Later, we see that Pharaoh trusted Joseph to run all of Egypt (Genesis 41:39-41).

God has entrusted us with the work of his kingdom. (1 Corinthians 4:1-2 & 1 Peter 4:10). We recognize that God has given us gifts, talents, and abilities. He has placed us where we can serve Him. We should recognize that as a great honor. We should also recognize that serving God gives meaning to life and offers great fulfillment. May he help us to faithfully fulfill our spiritual responsibilities.

<u>Day Thirteen</u>: Kneel to Pray for God's Blessings and Favor

The Old Testament tells us about a man named Jabez. 1 Chronicles 4 gives us a list of names. The writer mentions 44 people and suddenly stops to tell us about a man named Jabez. He was a man with a prayer request. It took only two verses with 33 words to give us a brief record of his prayer. His name means "pain and sorrow." Jabez was a man who wanted the blessings and favor of God. He asked God to bless him, and God answered his prayer.

We also need God's blessings and favor. The Bible assures us we can have them: Psalm 37:4 reads, "Delight thyself also in the Lord; and he shall give thee the desires of thine heart." Psalm 115:12a-15 tells us "The Lord hath been mindful of us: he will bless us… He will bless them that fear the Lord, both small and great. The Lord shall increase you more and more, you and your children. Ye are blessed of the Lord which made heaven and earth."

<u>Day Fourteen</u>: Kneel to Celebrate a Glorious Future

Do you remember the day you were saved? A Christian should look back and celebrate the love, grace, and mercy of God that brought forgiveness and salvation.

We should also celebrate the future God has promised us. Jesus went away to prepare a place for us (John 14:2-3). We are told that he wants to show us the exceeding riches of his grace in the ages to come (Ephesians 2:7). We bow before him with joy, thanksgiving, and great anticipation. We humbly ask him to help us be faithful to him as we finish our earthly journey.

WEEK THREE

This final week of prayer will focus upon our responsibility to pray for others. Jesus prayed for others when he said, "... as we forgive others." Hurting people surround us, bombarding us with requests to pray for them. We see the need to pray for others as we watch the nightly news. This week we will be reminded of this important aspect of prayer.

<u>Day Fifteen</u>: Kneel to Pray for Your Family

There was a man who watched his son endure great physical and mental pain. This father made his way to Jesus, knelt before him and asked the Lord to heal him. The Bible tells us his son was cured (Matthew 17:14-19). The father became an intercessor for his son, and his son received healing.

We, too, have the opportunity to be intercessors for our relatives. Let us take time to examine which of our family members are lost, which ones have sickness, disease, emotional issues, financial problems, addictions, or relationship problems. We kneel before the Lord and ask him to touch our families.

Day Sixteen: Kneel to Pray for Your Friends

Friends greatly enrich our lives. They are there for us when we go through setbacks and sorrows. And, we are there for them. Often friends may let us know about a hurt or need in their life. We have all seen the tears and painful expression of a friend who says, "Please pray for me." We recognize that our friend is struggling and needs our prayers.

As we pray we should think about the needs of our friends. Do we have a friend who has asked for prayer? Can we think of a friend who is hurting? Do we have a friend who is sick? Do we have a friend who is unemployed or in trouble financially? Do we have a friend who has strayed from God? The Bible tells us to "pray one for another" (James 5:16b).

Day Seventeen: Kneel to Pray for Spiritual Leaders

The church is the creation of Jesus Christ (Matthew 16:18). Jesus talked about something important that would happen within his church. He said, "My house shall be called the house of prayer" (Matthew 21:13b).

Spiritual leaders recognize that God has called and equipped them to serve (1 Corinthians 12 and Ephesians 4:11-13). They also recognize their great need for prayer support. Paul often asked for prayer (1 Thessalonians 5:25). The writer of Hebrews asked for prayer (Hebrews 13:18a). When Peter was arrested and jailed, the church responded with prayer. Peter received the miracle of being released (Acts 12:1-19). Spiritual leaders are leading the way in the warfare against spiritual wickedness in high places (Ephesians 6:12). As our leaders bravely stand against the enemy, they need our prayers.

<u>Day Eighteen</u>: Kneel to Pray for the Harvest

Did you know the Bible gives us specific things to pray about? One request says, "The harvest truly is great, but the labourers are few: pray ye therefore the Lord of the harvest, that he would send forth labourers into his harvest" (Luke 10:2b). We are given a prayer request from Jesus, telling us to pray that God would send laborers into the harvest field of the world.

Along with praying that God would send these laborers we should also pray for their protection. Missionaries around the world are in harm's way. These spiritual soldiers have risked their lives to take the gospel to others. They desperately need prayer support from the church. Let's be mindful of the importance of praying for those who have answered God's call to work in the harvest field.

Day Nineteen: Kneel to Pray
for Civic Leaders

Christian groups from across our nation are calling upon the church to pray for civic leaders. Those who are serving in local governments, schools, law enforcement, state governments, and other agencies and entities all need our prayers. We see violence, turmoil, and great divisions. Leaders struggle to make the right decisions and to meet needs with limited funds.

Paul let the church know that we have the responsibility to pray for those who lead. He wrote, "I exhort therefore, that, first of all, supplication, prayers, intercessions, and giving of thanks, be made for all men; For kings, and for all that are in authority..." (1 Timothy 2:1-2a).

Day Twenty: Kneel to Pray for America

One has only to read about the birth of America to understand that God has established this nation. A close study of our history as a nation reveals that God gave many miracles that led to our birth and survival.

On the other hand, one has only to observe the events that are happening in America today to see that our country is in deep trouble. We pledge that we are "One nation under God." We also proclaim, "In God We Trust" on our currency. Yet, we see our nation straying from God. We see our nation filled with violence, lawlessness, poverty, injustice, perversion, and other sins. We must pray that America will repent and return to him.

The Bible offers hope to any nation that will turn back to him (2 Chronicles 7:14). We must pray with great persistence. We must ask God to forgive us, to give us a revival, and to heal our land.

<u>Day Twenty-One</u>: Kneel to Pray for Jerusalem and the Nations

The Bible has another prayer request for us. We are to "Pray for the peace of Jerusalem" (Psalm 122:6a), a city that has seen constant turmoil. It has been a place of warfare and bloodshed throughout the centuries. It is still a place of unrest; however, one day in the future, it will be a place of peace, and the place from which Christ will reign on earth (Isaiah 24:23). Paul prayed for his nation of Israel (Romans 10:1). We must honor this biblical request and pray for Israel, too.

In other parts of the world we see political turmoil, health crises, humanitarian needs, natural disasters, and the need for the gospel. We should make this a matter of prayer. We must widen our scope of prayer beyond the needs of America and Israel.

David prayed, "God be merciful unto us, and bless us; and cause his face to shine upon us; Selah. That thy way may be known upon earth, thy saving health among all nations." (Psalm 67:1-2).

Part Two

Prayer School

"Now I lay me down to sleep. I pray the Lord
my soul to keep. If I should die before I wake.
I pray the Lord my soul to take."

****

"God is great, God is good. Let us thank Him
for this food. By His hands we all are fed.
Give us Lord our daily bread."

These two children's prayers remind us of lessons from
our childhood. They are the first prayers many children
learn. Remembering them gives us a good feeling about our
early life. However, some youngsters had no one to teach
them to pray, and they wish spiritual lessons had been a part
of growing up. Christian parents often begin early to teach
these prayers to their offspring. They want to help their
children learn how to talk to God. At meal times parents
often say, "Let's say the blessing before we eat." When going
to bed they often say, "Have you said your prayers?" These
parents are training their children to develop a prayer life.

Teaching spiritual lessons was part of God's educational plan for the children of Israel. Moses instructed parents to diligently teach their children the word of God, and to discuss God's word with them: while sitting in their homes, while walking, while going to bed, and while getting out of bed. He directed families to write the scriptures upon their homes, and to wear the scriptures on their bodies in small containers. This would remind them to never get away from what God had taught them (Deuteronomy 6:6-9).

The disciples had probably been trained in spiritual lessons as children. But, we might think that they had missed school or failed to learn their lessons when we read what they asked Jesus. They saw Jesus praying and asked, "Teach us to pray." (Luke 11:1). They must have sensed something deeper and different about the way Jesus prayed that inspired them to ask for such a prayer lesson. Jesus gave them an example of prayer, but also taught them many other lessons on the subject. They learned their lessons well. Following the ascension of Jesus, we see the disciples praying continually.

As with the disciples, we may also feel we need a prayer lesson. Parents and spiritual leaders have taught and encouraged us to pray. Yet, we acknowledge that our prayers often lack consistency and intensity. Sometimes it seems they are ineffective.

The book titled "*The Kneeling Christian*" has the story of ineffective prayers. The writer shared an incident he witnessed on a feast day in China. Worshippers went to their idol god in a sacred shrine. They carried handwritten prayers on small pieces of paper. They took the prayer and mixed it with mud--making a mud ball. They would fling the mud ball at their god. If the mud ball stuck, they believed their prayer would be answered.[1] The writer let us know they prayed to the wrong god, and they prayed in the wrong way. A little boy's prayer life is another good example of ineffective praying. He would write little prayer notes and throw them out the window. He hoped that the Lord would find his prayers.[2]

God's people have often felt inadequate in talking to God and in talking for God. Jeremiah felt a spiritual deficiency when called to be a prophet. God called him to speak to the nations. His response was, "I am just a child." (Jeremiah 1:6). God let him know he would be with him and help him. Moses felt this same spiritual deficiency. When called he said, "I am not eloquent ... I am slow of speech." (Exodus 4:10). We learn that God continued to teach Moses as he led the children of Israel. God said, "... will teach you what you shall do." (Exodus 4:15). We see that God allowed Aaron to serve as spokesman for Moses. God enabled both Jeremiah and Moses to be leaders. They learned how to pray and survive difficult situations.

God enables those who speak for him; and that ability comes through being able to speak to him. We desperately need to speak to him as we make our way through life. Solomon wrote, "In all thy ways acknowledge him, and he shall direct thy paths." (Proverbs 3:6). The Lord is still teaching us to pray. Sometimes we do not know what to pray for as we should. That is when the Holy Spirit assists us in our prayer lives (Romans 8:26). The disciples, Jeremiah, and Moses sought God's help through prayer, and so, should we.

An evangelist once shared the story of a prayer lesson he learned. When he arrived at a church for revival, he met the leader of the church prayer group. She was an older woman who walked with a cane. She approached the evangelist and asked, "Do you know how to pray?" He replied, "Yes." She told him to meet her for prayer early the next morning. As promised, he arrived on time and joined the small group. He discovered that their prayer time was unusually long. So, during prayer he placed his head on a chair and dozed off. She woke him by poking him with her cane. That week he discovered how to pray more effectively through her influence. Later, when she passed away, he was called upon to help with her memorial service. He held up her cane and asked a question: "Who will take the cane?"

We need to continue as students in the school of prayer. A teacher attends classes to be recertified to teach every few years. An auto mechanic attends classes to learn how to repair the newest cars. We, too, have lessons yet to learn to help us pray more effectively.

One great lesson relates to unanswered petitions. God admitted he will have a hearing problem if we fail to approach him the right way. The Bible tells us why some prayers are not heard.

1. Isaiah 59:2 - "But your iniquities have separated between you and your God, and your sins have hid his face from you, that he will not hear."

2. Jeremiah 7:16 - "Therefore pray not thou for this people, neither lift up cry nor prayer for them, neither make intercession to me: for I will not hear thee."

3. Psalm 66:18 - "If I regard iniquity in my heart, the Lord will not hear me."

When someone has a physical hearing problem, he schedules an appointment with a doctor, who administers a test to determine what is wrong. The doctor often recommends hearing aids to help restore a person's hearing. God told Israel how to correct his spiritual hearing.

2 Chronicles 7:14 - "If my people, which are called by my name, shall humble themselves, and pray, and seek my face, and turn from their wicked ways; then will I hear from heaven, and will forgive their sin, and will heal their land."

Israel's broken covenant with God had caused God to refuse to answer their prayers. He promised that their repentance would open his ears to hear their prayers. Our repenting from sin has the same result. Confessing and repenting of sins opens God's ears to our prayers. The word "abide" carries the same meaning. The branch abides in the vine to produce fruit. Jesus taught us that abiding in him causes God to hear and answer our prayers.

John 15:7 - "If ye abide in me, and my words abide in you, ye shall ask what ye will, and it shall be done unto you."

The Bible gives other reasons why prayer is not answered:

1. **Prayer that is offered with wrong motives**: James 4:3 - "Ye ask, and receive not, because ye ask amiss, that ye may consume it upon your lusts."

2. **Prayer that is contrary to His will**: 1 John 5:14b - "... if we ask any thing according to his will, he heareth us:"

3. **Prayer that is offered when there are relationship problems**: 1 Peter 3:7 - "Likewise, ye husbands, dwell with them according to knowledge, giving honour unto the wife, as unto the weaker vessel, and as being heirs together of the grace of life; that your prayers be not hindered."

4. **Prayer that is offered when we have unforgiveness in our hearts**: Matthew 5:23-24 - "Therefore if thou bring thy gift to the altar, and there rememberest that thy brother hath ought against thee…Leave there thy gift before the altar, and go thy way: first be reconciled to thy brother, and then come and offer thy gift."

5. **Prayer that is full of doubt**: James 1:6 - "But let him ask in faith, nothing wavering. For he that wavereth is like a wave of the sea driven with the wind and tossed."

6. **Prayer that is offered while living in disobedience**: 1 John 3:22 - "And whatsoever we ask, we receive of him, because we keep his commandments, and do those things that are pleasing in his sight."

7. **Prayer that has become a vain repetition**: <u>Matthew 6:7a</u> - "But when ye pray, use not vain repetitions, as the heathen do..."

8. **Prayer that is not offered in the name of Jesus**: <u>John 14:13-14</u> - "And whatsoever ye shall ask in my name, that will I do, that the Father may be glorified in the Son. If ye shall ask any thing in my name, I will do it."

There are two powerful examples of men praying and God not hearing them. The spiritual leaders of Israel thought they would be heard because they prayed long, religious prayers (Matthew 6:7). Jesus gave another example when he told about a man who went to the right place, but prayed the wrong way. He prayed a prayer filled with pride and self righteousness (Luke 18:9-14). There are many people like these men. They are sincere in their efforts to pray, but lack the spiritual knowledge to pray effectively. Though sincere prayers are offered to God, there is only heavenly silence. Prayer is to be a dialogue and not a monologue. God desires that his people would not only talk to him, but also listen to him.

Everyone who prays should acknowledge the need to learn how to pray more effectively. As we grow, we continue learning valuable lessons on prayer. Class is still in session for us. We desire to graduate one day. E.M. Bounds once said, "The house of God is a Divine workshop, and there the work of prayer goes on. Or the house of God is a Divine schoolhouse, in which the lesson of prayer is taught; where men and women learn to pray, and where they are graduated, in the school of prayer.[3]

Prayer Revival

The word "revival" often brings back memories from the past. Years ago an announcement would be made about a revival giving the name of the evangelist and the dates of the meetings. An evangelist with name recognition or a reputation for having wonderful revivals would stir up excitement and produce good attendance. The mindset seemed to be--pick the right preacher and the revival will be a success. The evangelist would preach or sing, and the hearts of the people would be moved. God would touch people's lives and perform miracles. The expectation and focus seemed to be on someone bringing a revival to the church, as if revival could be packed in the evangelist's luggage. Depending upon a pastor or evangelist to bring revival has produced a lot of good revivals, but a real reviving of our hearts is far more personal.

During the 1800's Rodney Gipsy Smith was an evangelist. He became a Christian at the age of 16. He taught himself to read and write, and loved to sing hymns. Some called him the "singing gypsy boy". Later, he became an evangelist, and would often break into song in the middle of his sermon. He crossed the Atlantic many times, and preached the gospel to hundreds of thousands. Everywhere he went a revival seemed to follow. He was once asked a question about how to have a revival. His answer reminds us that a real revival will always be a personal one. He said, "Go home. Lock yourself in your room. Kneel down in the middle of the floor, and with a piece of chalk draw a circle around yourself. There, on your knees, pray fervently and brokenly that God would start a revival within that chalk circle."

Booking an anointed evangelist is a great way to have a good revival. A better way is to follow the advice of Gipsy Smith. We must realize that a renewal of our commitment to God begins within us. We need not wait for church leadership to schedule it, or for a favorite evangelist to arrive. This awakening must first begin within our hearts. It will be personal, independent of the decision or the talent of others.

A personal revival begins by seeing a need for revival through a personal examination. When we have a health problem, we go to a doctor's office for a physical examination. The doctor asks questions, checks our weight, takes our temperature, checks our blood pressure and pulse rate. He may even listen to our lungs. If we have a physical problem, we may need medical treatment. The diagnosis of a health problem is startling and troubling. Facing the fact that something is seriously wrong is sobering. A doctor will often prescribe medicine, or give advice on making important physical changes. The changes a doctor suggest often require personal resolve and determination before we return to good health.

David saw a need for a spiritual examination. He cried, "Search me, O God, and know my heart: try me, and know my thoughts: And see if there be any wicked way in me, and lead me in the way everlasting." (Psalm 139:23-24). Paul recognized a need for members of the church at Corinth to examine themselves before partaking in communion. He said, "But let a man examine himself, and so let him eat of that bread, and drink of that cup."(1 Corinthians 11:28). We need a spiritual self-examination when we see the symptoms of spiritual illness.

A spiritual heart examination could reveal we are not healthy toward God. The results may show our spiritual life or vitality has vanished. Perhaps stuff has crowded God from our lives. Secret hidden sins may need to be confessed and forsaken. Serving God may have become a drudgery for us, rather than a delight. We may go through the motions of worship without really touching God. We may experience a loss of hunger and desire for spiritual things. We may have no joy or happiness within us. We may have no concern for the harvest. Once an examination reveals the symptoms of a spiritual heart problem, we will recognize that we need a personal revival.

The chalk circle lesson of Gipsy Smith is still important and relevant. It teaches us that a revival should always be personal. Salvation is a personal decision, as is, carrying our cross as a disciple of Christ. Participating in a 21-day Daniel fast is also a personal decision. Most chalk boards have been replaced by dry erase boards, or smart boards. A few places still sell chalk, but we need not buy chalk and draw a circle. Rather, we need to have the spiritual resolve and determination to get alone with God until we experience a personal revival.

Prayer Preparation

The familiar sound of the alarm clock signals the start of a new day. Families with children face the morning routine of getting the kids up, dressed, fed, and out the door for school. Later in the day, parents may take the kids to various activities. The end of the day brings homework and dinner. Soon everyone falls into bed exhausted. This is a typical scenario that reminds us that families are busy.

On Saturday, families may get to catch up on the loss of sleep from a hectic week. Everyone finds activities to do to relax. On Sunday morning, the family gets ready for church, where the pastor may preach a sermon on the importance of prayer. Parents listen and feel guilty. Their minds may drift to their many responsibilities and obligations. They may make a mental note that says, "We need to find time to pray."

Finding time for a vibrant prayer life presents a challenge. I'm reminded of a busy mother who had a strange way of making time for prayer. Her name was Susanna Wesley. She had nineteen children, but nine died as infants. Her husband was unreliable. She discovered that praying was the only way she could meet the many demands upon her life. A house full of kids made it difficult to find a place to get alone and pray. So when she wanted to get alone with God, she would simply lift her apron over her head. Her children knew that this meant mom was praying, and they left her alone. Her prayers so influenced her sons John and Charles Wesley that they became mighty men of God.

Like Susanna, we may be busy and over obligated, but we must recognize the importance of making time for prayer. Time spent with God will renew us and give us strength. The Bible reminds us about being still in his presence, and of taking time to wait upon him.

1. Psalm 46:10a - "Be still, and know that I am God..."
2. Isaiah 40:31- "But they that wait upon the Lord shall renew their strength; they shall mount up with wings as eagles; they shall run, and not be weary; and they shall walk, and not faint."

Nothing can replace the power and strength we receive by being still and waiting before him in prayer.

Jesus once spoke to Peter about spending time in prayer. Jesus was desperately praying to the Father asking that the cup pass from him. He had prayed with such fervor and intensity that his sweat became as great drops of blood falling to the ground. The disciples often slept through some important moments. This time Jesus went to a sleepy Simon Peter and said to him in Matthew 26:40b, "What, could ye not watch with me one hour?" An hour is a short time, but Peter was too drowsy to witness the prayer of Jesus, or to support him in his hour of need. May we always find time to intercede for others through a consistent and fruitful prayer life.

Once we make time to pray, we should then consider how to make that time more meaningful. Praying can become routine, or it can be exciting, adventurous, and new. We should come before God with anticipation. Consider the following questions before approaching God in prayer:

1. How will the Holy Spirit prompt or inspire me to pray today?
2. Will God speak a special word into my heart?
3. Will my prayer influence help a missionary today?
4. Will my prayer influence lead to a miracle today?
5. Will my day change after I pray as God provides or protects me?
6. What words of worship will I use as I pray?
7. How will he touch me today--my mind, my body, or my spirit?
8. Will he reveal a special task for me to accomplish?
9. Will I feel his love or power?
10. Will he speak many things into my heart, or be silent today?
11. Will my prayer be the reason a family member receives healing or strength?
12. Will I be given more understanding about a scripture?
13. Will he confront and reveal carnality in my heart so I can repent?
14. Will I sense his holiness?

15. Will my prayers for the person in the hospital be the reason the great physician walks into the room?
16. Who has asked me to pray for them?
17. What did the Bible tell me to pray for?
18. Will I receive a special burden to pray for someone?
19. Will God give me understanding, wisdom, or guidance?
20. What is happening in the news that I should pray about?

We should approach prayer in a practical way. Find a good and comfortable place to pray, removing any hindrances. Determine what tasks should be accomplished before prayer, and what can be put off until later. Clear your mind of all distractions by being silent before God for a few minutes. Make a list of people who need prayer. These things require preparation.

We should prepare before we pray. The worship within the old testament tabernacle serves as a good example of preparing to approach God. God told Moses to make a sanctuary that he might dwell among them (Exodus 25:8). The Lord gave specific instructions regarding how they were to approach him. These instructions were detailed and specific. The animals that would become sacrifices had to be inspected. The blood had to be caught and applied in a prescribed way. The shewbread had to be prepared and placed on the table just as God had instructed. Priests had to wash before approaching God. Priests washing themselves before going into the tabernacle reminds us of Psalm 24:1-2b. "Who shall ascend into the hill of the Lord? or who shall stand in his holy place? He that hath clean hands, and a pure heart."

Among the many things being prepared for worship was the incense. It was made from sweet spices (Exodus 30:34). The incense was a perfume for the altar of incense (Exodus 30:37). It took time to collect and mix these ingredients. This perfume confection was placed on the altar of incense as the priest approached God (Exodus 40:26-27). The sweet smell of this incense speaks to us of our prayers ascending to God. David sang, "Let my prayer be set forth before thee as incense" (Psalm 141:2).

Preparations makes our prayers more specific and much more effective. Our prayers will have greater results and more power. Preparing our heart to pray will move the hand of God. We will have influence in the heavens, and see intervention on earth. We should remember that God delights in answering prayer. His word has encouraged us to ask, seek, and knock (Matthew 7:7), to call upon him (Jeremiah 33:3), and he even said something astounding: "Command ye me" (Isaiah 45:11).

It was once said that a minister was given the privilege of praying with a man known as "praying Hyde". This man was known to stay in prayer for days until he knew God had answered his prayer. The two entered a room to pray. Both men got down on their knees. Praying Hyde did not utter a word for about five minutes. He knelt, preparing his heart in silence. He finally said, "O God." Then he was still again. This great prayer warrior knew when he had established a connection. Then, he offered great petitions to God.

Prayer Purpose

No one likes confrontation. To face someone making distressing comments is difficult. Criticism causes us to examine the merit of what is being said. Prayer warrior E.M. Bounds once shared an illustration about an encounter not with a person, but with God. This confrontation related to a person's prayer life. Bounds pictured God, somehow grabbing a person by the shirt as he or she finished praying. He then imagined what God might ask: "What did you pray for in your prayer closet?"[4] Many people, quite honestly, would have a hard time answering. This means the time of prayer lacked specificity and purpose. Would you have a response, if this happened to you? James shared a surprising revelation about unanswered prayer. James 4:3 says, "Ye ask and receive not because you ask amiss..."

God once asked Solomon to be specific in what he desired. Solomon had the ultimate dream. God appeared and encouraged him to request what he wanted, saying, "Ask what I shall give thee." (1 Kings 3:5). We wonder how long it took Solomon to answer, and what he considered before deciding. Solomon asked God for an explicit request. He wanted wisdom to reign. God granted his petition and was so pleased that he also lavished other blessings upon him (1 Kings 4:29-34).

Jesus often questioned people about their exact need. When blind Bartimaeus stood before him, Jesus asked, "What wilt thou that I should do unto thee?" (Mark 10:51). Bartimaeus had no trouble being precise. He wanted to receive his sight. God granted him his miracle. The mother of James and John brought a petition to Jesus. Being a mother she wanted the best for her sons. Jesus asked her, "What wilt thou?" (Matthew 20:21). She requested that her sons be given the honor of sitting on his right and left when Jesus reigns. Jesus let her know that she did not understand what she was asking. Though the Lord knew the thoughts and needs of those around him, he still wanted people to state what they wanted.

A missionary once told the story of wanting and needing a bicycle. He prayed a vague prayer asking for one. He did not receive the bicycle. He then discovered that the Lord wanted him to pray in specifics. He offered a prayer for the kind of bicycle he desired. The next day he received the exact bicycle he had requested.

A family decided to take a drive into the mountains. It was a day trip just to get away for a little while. A young girl asked to go with them. They drove through the beautiful North Carolina mountains that day. They came upon a small country store and purchased items to make bologna sandwiches for lunch. Driving back home the little girl wanted to know why they went to the mountains. The father, known to have a great sense of humor, said, "Oh, we like to drive up into the mountains just to get a bologna sandwich." The family was looking for relaxation, the little girl was looking for purpose.

The many recorded prayers of the Bible show people praying with a purpose. Notice these examples of specific prayer:

1. Abram was childless and asked God to help him (Genesis 15:2-4).
2. Jacob wrestled on the ground with an angel. He refused to let go until he received his blessing (Genesis 32:26).
3. Hannah prayed that God would give her a son (1 Samuel 1:11).
4. Jabaz prayed that God would bless and enlarge him (1 Chronicles 4:10).
5. David prayed for direction to fight the enemy (2 Samuel 5:19/23).
6. David prayed that God would turn the counsel of Ahithophil (2 Samuel 15:31).
7. Hezekiah prayed that God would deliver Judah from Sennacherib (Isaiah 37:15-20).
8. Daniel fasted and prayed for 21 days to know the future of his people (Daniel 10:2-3).
9. Jesus taught a parable about a woman who had been treated unjustly. She persistently sought for justice (Luke 18:2-5).
10. In another parable, Jesus taught about a man who needed bread for a late night traveler. He went to a friend and specifically asked for bread (Luke 11:5-10).

Far too many times we have approached God and offered prayers that are too vague or too general. We have all prayed, "Lord would you touch her." "Father, would you bless him." Although these prayers are good, they fail to spell out what we need God to do. He wants to grant our petitions. He receives worship, honor, and glory after he answers our prayers.

Prayer Posture

The window faced toward Jerusalem. This window was opened three times every day for a specific reason: Daniel had chosen that place for daily prayer. One would think Daniel's life of devotion to God would be admired and appreciated; but instead, it created dangerous enemies. From the outside one would not only have seen the open window, but also a group of men lurking beneath it assembled to try to catch Daniel praying.

To discover someone at prayer should be praiseworthy. However, these men were looking for a way to destroy Daniel. Being his associates under King Cyrus, they had already talked the king into punishing anyone who offered a petition in any name but the king's. Daniel knew about the new decree from the king. He knew praying could jeopardize his life. He chose to continue to pray whatever the outcome. These men now had the proof they needed.

The king heard the evidence and though it made him sad, he had no choice but to pass sentence on Daniel. His crime was serious; punishment was death. So this great prayer warrior was placed in the den of lions. The king recognized his mistake in signing the decree, especially because Daniel was a friend. He walked the floor as the night slowly passed. Early the next morning the king hastily made his way to Daniel and with a lamentable voice he cried, "O Daniel, servant of the living God, is thy God, whom thou servest continually, able to deliver thee from the lions?" (Daniel 6:20b). Daniel replied, "My God hath sent his angel, and hath shut the lions' mouths..." (Daniel 6:22a). The king had Daniel taken from the lions' den and then placed Daniel's enemies there.

We see Daniel in this story praying three times a day upon his knees. We know a lot about the life of Daniel. One thing we do not know is who taught Daniel to pray? We assume it was his parents. The instructions he had received on prayer had stuck with him throughout life. We notice an important prayer position that Daniel used. He had the custom of praying three times a day on his knees. History has revealed that many Jewish men stood praying with their arms out, and their palms uplifted. Daniel was one of many who wanted to kneel.

To bow down on your knees before a person of authority is an act of submission. Throughout history kneeling has been a position that shows respect, reverence, and humility to those in authority. The rich young ruler ran to Jesus. He showed respect by kneeling before him. He wanted to know how to receive eternal life (Mark 10:17). Many have knelt for the purpose of receiving mercy, such as a desperate father. Matthew wrote, "And when they were come to the multitude, there came to him a certain man, kneeling down to him, and saying, Lord, have mercy on my son..." (Matthew 17:14-15a). Jesus graciously healed this sick boy.

Bible history shows others bowing down for different reasons. Ezra, for instance said, "And at the evening sacrifice I arose up from my heaviness; and having rent my garment and my mantle, I fell upon my knees, and spread out my hands unto the Lord my God." (Ezra 9:5). King Solomon knelt before God to pray for God's blessings upon Israel (2 Chronicles 6:13); while Peter went to his knees and saw the miracle of Tabitha being raised from the dead (Acts 9:40). Stephen, as he took his final breath, "kneeled down, and cried with a loud voice, Lord, lay not this sin to their charge." (Acts 7:60). Paul bent his knees on a prison floor and prayed for the saints at Ephesus (Ephesians 3:14). Jesus knelt and prayed three times for the cup to pass from him (Luke 22:41).

Tragically, one group of soldiers knelt before Jesus to disrespect Him. Matthew shared the horrific details, "And when they platted a crown of thorns, they put it upon his head, and a reed in his right hand: and they bowed the knee before him, and mocked him, saying, Hail, King of the Jews!" (Matthew 27:29).

Ironically, they will one day have to kneel again, but for a different reason. The Bible says, "Wherefore God also hath highly exalted him, and given him a name which is above every name: That at the name of Jesus every knee should bow, of things in heaven, and things in earth, and things under the earth." (Philippians 2:9-10). All those who have rejected and fought against God will one day kneel before him. Mary was a woman who had the right understanding of worshipping the Lord. Three times she is seen at the feet of Jesus. John tells us she loved and worshipped the Lord by bowing at his feet to anoint him.

Paul wrote about everyone bowing before God and quoted the Old Testament. He wrote, "For it is written, As I live, saith the Lord, every knee shall bow to me, and every tongue shall confess to God" (Romans 14:11). To bow your knees before God in prayer shows submission, reverence, and humility. It is also a wonderful way to worship and offer up your petitions. The psalmist wrote, "O Come, let us worship and bow down: let us kneel before the Lord our maker" (Psalm 95:6).

Daniel was a man who prayed three times a day on his knees. His consistent prayer life resulted in God giving him the miracle of deliverance. Consider the following testimonies and stories of those who have influenced others by praying on their knees. Edward Payson was a pastor who was known as an intercessor. He kneeled in a certain place to pray very often, and tarried long. E.M. Bounds said, "He wore the hard-wood boards into grooves where his knees pressed so often and long."[5]

- David Livingstone was a man of prayer. He died the way he lived. They found him dead upon his knees.[6]
- Whitefield says, "Whole days and weeks have I spent prostrate on the ground, in silent prayer,' Fall upon your knees, and grow there,' is the language of another, who knew that whereof he affirmed."[7]

- Isaac Newton once said, "I can take my telescope and look millions of miles into space; but I can lay my telescope aside, get down on my knees in earnest prayer, and I can see more of heaven and get closer to God than I can when assisted by all the telescopes and material agencies on earth."[8]

- The doctor said, "Sir, you cannot live more than one-half hour." The response was surprising. The patient said, "Then take me out of bed and place me on my knees! Let me spend the time in prayer for this sinful world."[9]

- Cromwell believed in much praying upon his knees. Looking on one occasion at the statues of famous men, he turned to a friend and said: "Make mine kneeling, for thus I came to glory."[10]

- Constantine saw other coins with proud Emperors standing. He said, "Make my coin kneeling."[11]

- James prayed so often on his knees that he was called, Old Camel Knees.[12]

- George Washington travailed in prayer on his knees at Valley Forge.

- Fanny Crosby would not attempt to write a song until she had prayed on her knees.

- The first thing Queen Victoria did as the new queen was to get on her knees and ask God to help her.

- The last thing many did in the Twin Towers on September, 11, 2001, was to kneel together in prayer. Many accepted Christ just before the building collapsed.

These testimonies and stories remind us that miracles can happen when we kneel and pray. An old adage says, "Prayer changes things!" Consider these changes that can happen as a result of praying on our knees:

- ❖ Sinners become saints
- ❖ Darkness becomes light
- ❖ Defeat becomes victory
- ❖ Weakness becomes strength
- ❖ Despair becomes hope
- ❖ Sickness becomes health
- ❖ Poverty becomes plenty
- ❖ Inability becomes giftedness
- ❖ The impossible becomes possible
- ❖ Fear becomes courage
- ❖ Bondage becomes liberty
- ❖ The lowly become the lifted
- ❖ The hindered become the advanced
- ❖ The fractured become the mended
- ❖ A barrenness becomes a harvest

Prayer Closet

A closet could be described as a small, dusty, crowded place for shoes, clothes, and storage. Potential homebuyers may notice the number of closets, as well as, their location. We usually open ours in the morning to decide what to wear. Then, it often stays closed until the following morning. The closet is one place in our home that usually needs attention. It may contain old clothes and old shoes, along with other things that need to be discarded.

Jesus talked about a closet in his sermon on the mount. He said, "But thou, when thou prayest, enter into thy closet, and when thou hast shut thy door, pray to thy Father which is in secret; and thy Father which seeth in secret shall reward thee openly" (Matthew 6:6). He used the closet to teach a lesson about prayer. Everyone should have a private place where they can get alone with God.

Daniel liked to pray toward Jerusalem before his open window. One Christian everyone knew as "Bob", had a whole room with an altar for prayer. Some pray in different rooms in their home: perhaps in the bedroom, maybe in the living room or den, or in the sunroom that overlooks the outdoors. It is important to have a location for secret times of prayer.

A great many Christians have never selected a special place for prayer. They usually offer a quick prayer to God while driving to work. Those prayer petitions are often focused on asking God for his help with the tasks that are to be faced during the day. In times of trouble or a crisis, their prayers become more intensified. Once the emergency is over, they revert back to their former routine of prayer. It is tough to have a good prayer life doing 55 miles per hour, maneuvering through traffic, and stopping for red lights. We all face situations when we must intercede while on the go, but if on-the-go prayers are our norm, our relationship with God will be deficient.

A prayer closet regimen is essential to face principalities and powers, rulers of darkness, and spiritual wickedness in high places. We must pray as we face the demands and stress of life. An unfriendly, unholy, culture that has rejected God surrounds us, and we must stand against the wiles of the devil and withstand evil. We have decisions to make that greatly affect our lives and our families. For these reasons, a prayer closet relationship with God is imperative.

The prayer closet is that secret place the author of Psalm 91, sang about: "He that dwelleth in the secret place of the most High shall abide under the shadow of the Almighty" (Psalm 91:1). To dwell is to establish ourselves in his presence. It is to abide in him (John 15:1-8). Jesus let us know that abiding or dwelling in God is essential for experiencing answered prayer. He said, "If ye abide in me, and my words abide in you, ye shall ask what ye will, and it shall be done unto you" (John 15:7).

Not only will we experience answered prayer through dwelling in the secret place, but we will experience incredible fellowship with God. We know that God abides within us (John 14:23). He has chosen to fellowship with us through prayer. It may surprise you, but God enjoys your company. He seeks for people to worship him (John 4:23). A young man sat with his family one evening enjoying Christmas. Suddenly, a still small voice within spoke, "Come outside, I want to spend some time with you!" He quietly got up and left the room unnoticed. Outside in the dark, he stopped under a big oak tree. There he prayed and experienced God's wonderful presence, and was spiritually refreshed. We might expect a friend to call us and say, "Let's get together. We haven't talked in a long time." We do not expect God to initiate a meeting, but he has initiated or called for us to meet with him many times. The words of Jesus still beckon us to enter his presence. "Come unto me," Jesus said, (Matthew 11:28). The author of Hebrews also let us know we have the invitation to come to him. The Bible says, "Let us therefore come boldly unto the throne of grace..." (Hebrews 4:16a). Fellowship with God is awaiting us in our prayer closet.

The first obstacle we face in establishing a prayer schedule will be seen when we look in the mirror. The person staring back at us may lack the discipline, so we must fight the first battle with self. Paul said, "For the flesh lusteth against the Spirit, and the Spirit against the flesh: and these are contrary the one to the other: so that ye cannot do the things that ye would." (Galatians 5:17). We acknowledge that sitting with the remote, standing with a fishing pole or golf club, or riding a motorcycle is more fun than travailing in a prayer closet. Finding ways to relax and enjoy life are important, but we are not to neglect our spiritual need for prayer. We are to walk in the Spirit, and not fulfill the lust of the flesh (Galatians 5:16).

The prayer closet has many spiritual dimensions. There we offer prayers for different needs and situations. There we face the carnality within us. This dimension of prayer reminds us of the potter's wheel. The potter found the clay on his wheel was marred, so he made it again into another vessel that pleased him. (Jeremiah 18:4). In our place of prayer God cleanses us and forms us into a vessel that he can use. We are, in fact, to be formed into the image of Jesus Christ (Romans 8:29). Here we are made into a living sacrifice unto God (Romans 12:1). This is where we put on the belt of truth (Ephesians 6:14). Here we worship God in spirit and in truth (John 4:23). This is the place where secret sins are removed, and we are reformed by God's grace.

A personal revival begins with a pliable heart. As we pray, God works in our lives to change us. A prominent pastor once talked about how the prayer closet changes us. He said something like this. "We find ourselves weighed down by burdens, and surrounded by troubles. We go into our prayer closets. God touches us. We come out different. We emerge changed. Now, have the hard situations changed? Have the problems been solved? No, the circumstances around us may remain the same, but God has done a work within us. He has revived us and given us strength to meet the challenges." This wonderful spiritual and emotional change happens when we make our way into his presence.

The prayer closet provides a place of submission to his will, where God calls us and displays his grace by giving us gifts. It is a place where our lives are changed, as we receive direction for our lives. We often enter a time of prayer struggling with important decisions about the future. His word reminds us that he will direct our steps (Psalm 37:23). And, as we pray, he will direct our paths (Proverb 3:5-6).

Those who enter a prayer closet are sometimes called "prayer warriors". The prayer closet has been referred to as a "war room". Warriors in the war room know a real war is raging. Warriors recognize that Jesus actually won the war when he died on Calvary. Paul told us about a magnificent scene of Jesus being triumphant over the devil. He said, "And having spoiled principalities and powers, he made a shew of them openly, triumphing over them in it" (Colossians 2:15). This powerful declaration lets us know the war is over, and the outcome is certain (Revelation 20:10). Spiritual warriors know that in spite of the war being won, spiritual battles are still being waged. We also know that the church has been given power over our enemy (Luke 10:19). The church rejoices because Jesus lives within us, and "greater is He that is in you, than he that is in the world" (1 John 4:4b). God instructs us to resist the devil, stand against him, and pull down his strongholds (2 Corinthians 10:4-5). Prayer is the key to evicting the devil from any area where he has a stronghold.

E.M. Bounds wrote about this warfare saying, "It cannot be stated too frequently that the life of a Christian is a warfare, an intense conflict, a lifelong contest. It is a battle, moreover, waged against invisible foes, who are alert, and ever seeking to entrap, deceive, and ruin the souls of men."[13] He also said that many Christians are unaware of the conflict: "How little the average church member appears to know of the character of the conflict, and of its demands upon him!"[14] Battles are won and lost according to what happens in the prayer closet. Dr. Benny Beckum has said, "The secret prayer chamber is a bloody battleground. Here violent and decisive battles are fought out."[15]

"Prayer is our most formidable weapon", says E.M. Bounds, "but the one in which we are the least skilled, the most averse to its use."[16] Would any soldier ever enter combat without being taught how to use a weapon? Prayer is indeed a great and powerful weapon to our warfare against the enemy.

The Saxon king of Northumberland invaded Wales. His army was about to battle the Britons when he saw a host of unarmed men. He asked who they were and what they were doing. They told him they were monks praying for the success of their countrymen. The king said, "They have begun the fight against us; attack them first."[17]

A king named "Hezekiah" witnessed an invasion of the Assyrian army. He was not in a position to defend himself, or to defeat the enemy. He was so distraught that he tore his clothes in anguish and put on sack cloth (Isaiah 37:1). He had one and only one option. He went to the house of the

Lord and prayed. He may have not had swords or soldiers enough to defeat the enemy, but he knew how to pray. He lay down on the floor and offered a powerful prayer asking God to save them. God responded, sending the prophet Isaiah to give him an answer to his prayer. God assured the king that the enemy would not destroy the city, but that God would defend it (Isaiah 37:35). Only one angel of God was dispatched to fight for Judah, and he annihilated the army of the Assyrians in one night. There are awesome times when God suddenly intervenes when we pray.

A king named "Jehoshaphat" also experienced victory when he prayed. A mighty host from several countries came up against Judah. The king proclaimed a fast to seek God for deliverance. The Lord stepped in and a prophet said, "... the battle is not your's, but God's," (2 Chronicles 20:15c).

There are times that we enter our prayer closet to battle for others. A Virginia evangelist once shared an inspirational story about entering his prayer closet to pray for a friend who had great difficulties. The evangelist was a 16-year old high school student at the time. He was upstairs doing his homework when he heard someone come into his parents home. His mother started praying with a woman downstairs below his room. He put down his pencil and started praying with them. He said, "It was as if their prayers were passing through my bedroom on the way to heaven." He decided to join them. His mother was in one corner praying. The woman with the difficulties was in another corner praying. So, he choose another corner. They prayed about 15 more minutes. The woman told him about some of the tragedies in her family and about her financial trouble. She had hit rock bottom.

The young evangelist began to tell her about a dream he had about her. He said, "I saw you walking down a path through the woods. It was a nice day. You were taking a leisurely walk and enjoying yourself. I saw a storm that arose behind you. You were frightened and started walking faster. The wind began to swirl and a small tree fell over in front of you. It didn't stop you, but you did slow a little, and then you stepped over it. You became more frightened and you ran at a frantic pace. Then, a larger tree fell in front of you across the path; you couldn't step over it, so you had to climb over it. You continued to run as fast as you could. Finally, a huge tree fell across the path, and you couldn't go over it, under it, or around it. I saw you raise your hands, close your eyes, and pray. I saw you, in faith, take a step and your leg disappeared into the tree. You walked through the tree, and I saw you come out on the other side."

That woman began to rejoice. God did bring her through those hard places. Decades have passed since the dream. When she sees the evangelist she mentions that dream. She has also told him that God has taken her through many hard places that could have been stopping points in her life, but she is still going forward. Mighty revelations, breakthroughs, and miracles happen when we enter our prayer closet.[18]

The prophet Daniel was a man who fasted and prayed for others as well. He prayed, confessing the sins of his people (Daniel 9:5). He prayed and acknowledged the great confusion that his people were enduring (Daniel 9:7-8). He fasted and mourned for three weeks. (Daniel 10:2-3). In Daniel chapter 10, he prayed by the side of a great river. There he received a vision, an angelic visitation, a revelation about the enemy fighting against him, a supernatural touch that gave him strength, and the answer to his fasting and prayer.

Our nations, our churches, our families, our friends, and we, ourselves, need to fast and pray. God is looking for people who will stand in the gap as prayer warriors. Daniel's times of fasting and prayer have inspired us. Each year many of us emulate him by entering into a 21-day Daniel fast.

Our prayer is that this Daniel fast prayer guide helps you maintain spiritual focus during your Daniel fast, and that you do experience a personal revival.

Endnotes

1   Unknown Christian, *The Kneeling Christian* (Middletown, DE, 2014), 4.

2   Austin Phelps, *The Still Hour or Communion With God* (CURIOSMITH, MN, 2011), 49.

3   E.M. Bounds, *The Necessity of Prayer* (Grand Rapids, MI, 1982), 140.

4   E.M. Bounds, *The Purpose in Prayer* (Grand Rapids, MI, 1982), 118.

5   Dr. Benny Beckum, *Prayer for Revival* (Statesboro, GA: Intercessor Ministries, Inc. 2008), 67.

6   E.M. Bounds, *The Purpose in Prayer* (Grand Rapids, MI, 1982), 42.

7   Austin Phelps, *The Still Hour or Communion With God* (CURIOSMITH, MN, 2011), 50.

8   Lowell Lundstrom, *How You Can Pray with Power and Get Results* (Sisseton SD, 1981), 6.

9   Ibid., 53.

10 E.M. Bounds, *The Purpose in Prayer* (Grand Rapids, MI, 1982), 21.

11 C.H. Spurgeon, *True Prayer True Power* (A sermon delivered at Exeter Hall, Strand, on August, 12, 1860).

12 Herbert Lockyer, *All The Prayers Of the Bible* (Grand Rapids, MI: Zondervan Pubishing House, 1959), 265.

13 E.M. Bounds, *The Necessity Of Prayer* (Grand Rapids, MI, 1982),109.

14 Ibid., 110.

15 Dr. Benny Beckum, *Prayer for Revival* (Statesboro, GA: Intercessor Ministries, Inc. 2008), 173.

16 E.M. Bounds, *The Purpose in Prayer* (Grand Rapids, MI, 1982), 48.

17 Austin Phelps, *The Still Hour or Communion With God* (CURIOSMITH, MN, 2011), 22-23.

18 Clifton West, *Now Will I Praise the Lord* (A sermon delivered at Soul's Harbor Church of God, Manassas, Virginia).